SECRETS OF THE ANIMAL WORLD

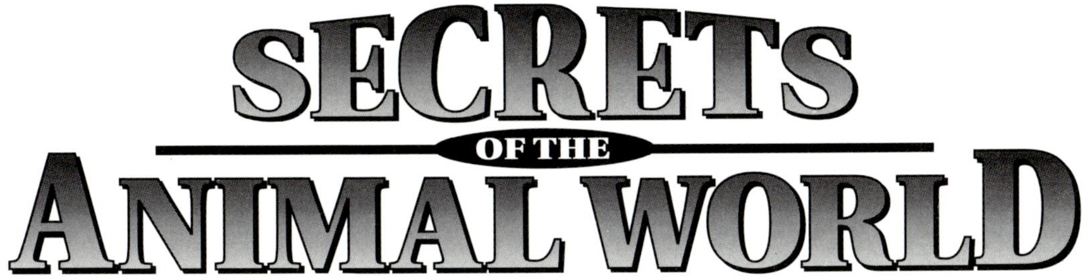

ANTS
A Great Community

by Andreu Llamas
Illustrated by Gabriel Casadevall and Ali Garousi

Gareth Stevens Publishing
MILWAUKEE

For a free color catalog describing Gareth Stevens' list of high-quality books, call 1-800-542-2595 (USA) or 1-800-461-9120 (Canada). Gareth Stevens' Fax: (414) 225-0377.

The editor would like to extend special thanks to Jan W. Rafert, Curator of Primates and Small Mammals, Milwaukee County Zoo, Milwaukee, Wisconsin, for his kind and professional help with the information in this book.

Library of Congress Cataloging-in-Publication Data

Llamas, Andreu.
    [Hormiga. English]
    Ants: a great community / by Andreu Llamas; illustrated by Gabriel Casadevall and
  Ali Garousi.
       p. cm. — (Secrets of the animal world)
    Includes bibliographical references (p.) and index.
    Summary: Provides detailed descriptions of the physical characteristics and behavior
  of ants.
    ISBN 0-8368-1393-6 (lib. bdg.)
    1. Ants—Juvenile literature. [1. Ants.] I. Casadevall, Gabriel, ill. II. Garousi,
  Ali, ill. III. Title. IV. Series.
  QL568.F7L6213 1996
  595.79'6—dc20
                                           95-45837

This North American edition first published in 1996 by
Gareth Stevens Publishing
1555 North RiverCenter Drive, Suite 201
Milwaukee, Wisconsin 53212 USA

This U.S. edition © 1996 by Gareth Stevens, Inc. Created with original © 1993 Ediciones Este, S.A., Barcelona, Spain. Additional end matter © 1996 by Gareth Stevens, Inc.

Series editor: Patricia Lantier-Sampon
Editorial assistants: Diane Laska, Rita Reitci, Derek Smith

Printed in the United States of America

1 2 3 4 5 6 7 8 9 99 98 97 96

CONTENTS

THE WORLD OF ANTS

Where ants live

Ants belong to the order Hymenoptera, which includes over 103,000 different insect species. Because of their unique way of life, ants can live in practically every corner of the world, from mountaintops to prairies. They can survive in every kind of environment, including deserts. It should come as no surprise, therefore, that ants have made their homes in city gardens and even in our homes.

Sometimes we can find colonies of ants living in our homes.

Most types of ants live in warm, tropical regions.

Life in a colony

Ants live in highly organized colonies that often number over a million individuals. Each ant has a specific task, and all ants work together for the survival of the colony.

Ants have a special language for communication: they exchange rhythmic antenna signals. They also send and detect chemical substances that help them recognize each other and warn of coming danger.

Ants are so strong they can carry objects that are much heavier than they are over very long distances.

Workers must exchange signals with a sentry to enter the nest.

Many types of ants

There are over 8,800 species of ants that vary greatly in size and physical appearance. Ant families differ mainly in their physical characteristics, such as the shape of their head, thorax, and abdomen. Each species has a different lifestyle. Two examples of this are harvester ants that store grain in

Myrmica worker (bulldog ant) Length: 0.16-0.28 inches (4-7 mm). It lives in grass and prefers damp areas.

Ponera worker (ponerid ant) Length: 0.1-0.14 inches (2.5-3.5 mm). It lives under rocks in narrow tunnels.

Leptanilla male (migratory ant) Length: 0.04-0.05 inch (1-1.3 mm)

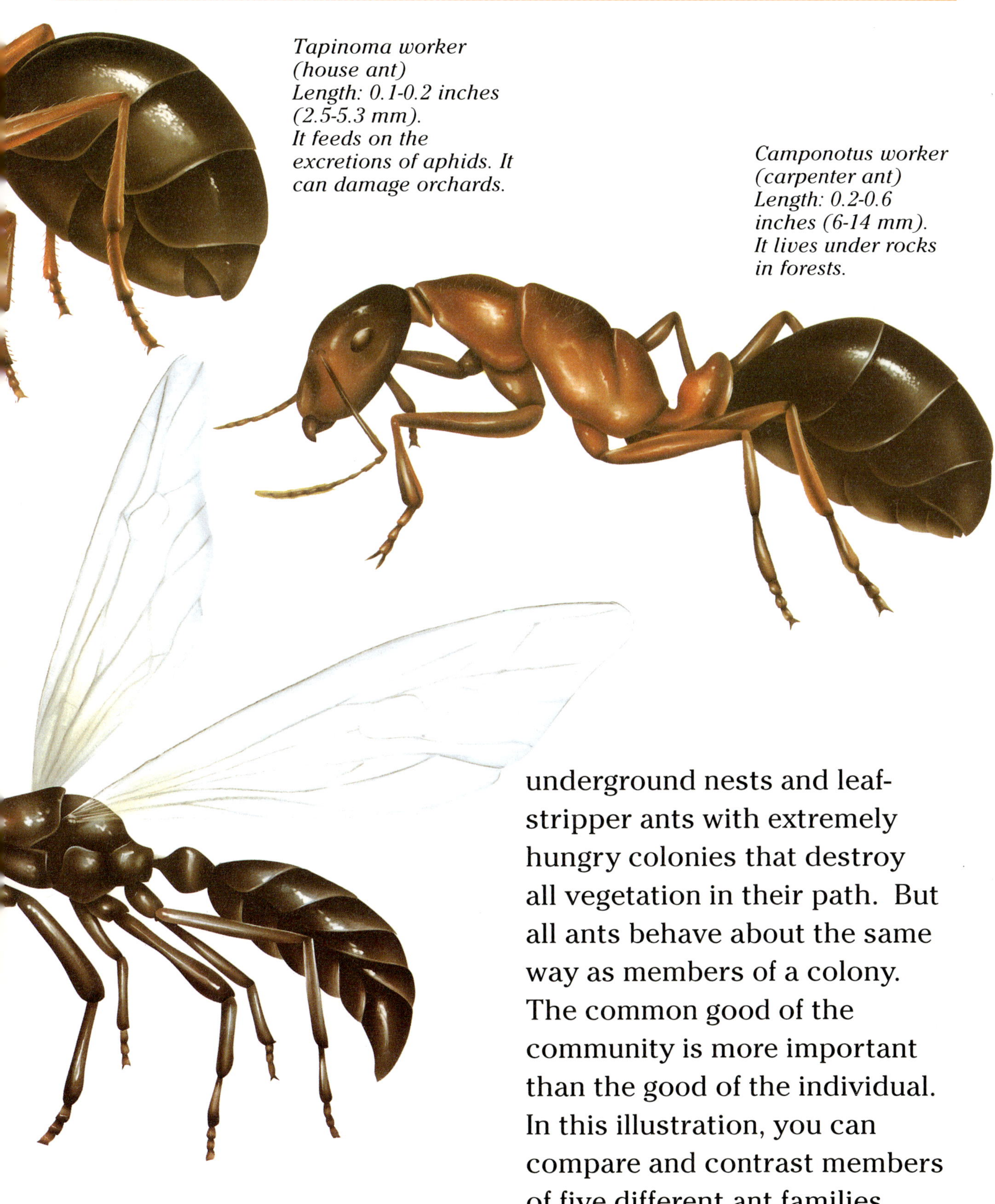

underground nests and leaf-stripper ants with extremely hungry colonies that destroy all vegetation in their path. But all ants behave about the same way as members of a colony. The common good of the community is more important than the good of the individual. In this illustration, you can compare and contrast members of five different ant families.

INSIDE THE ANT

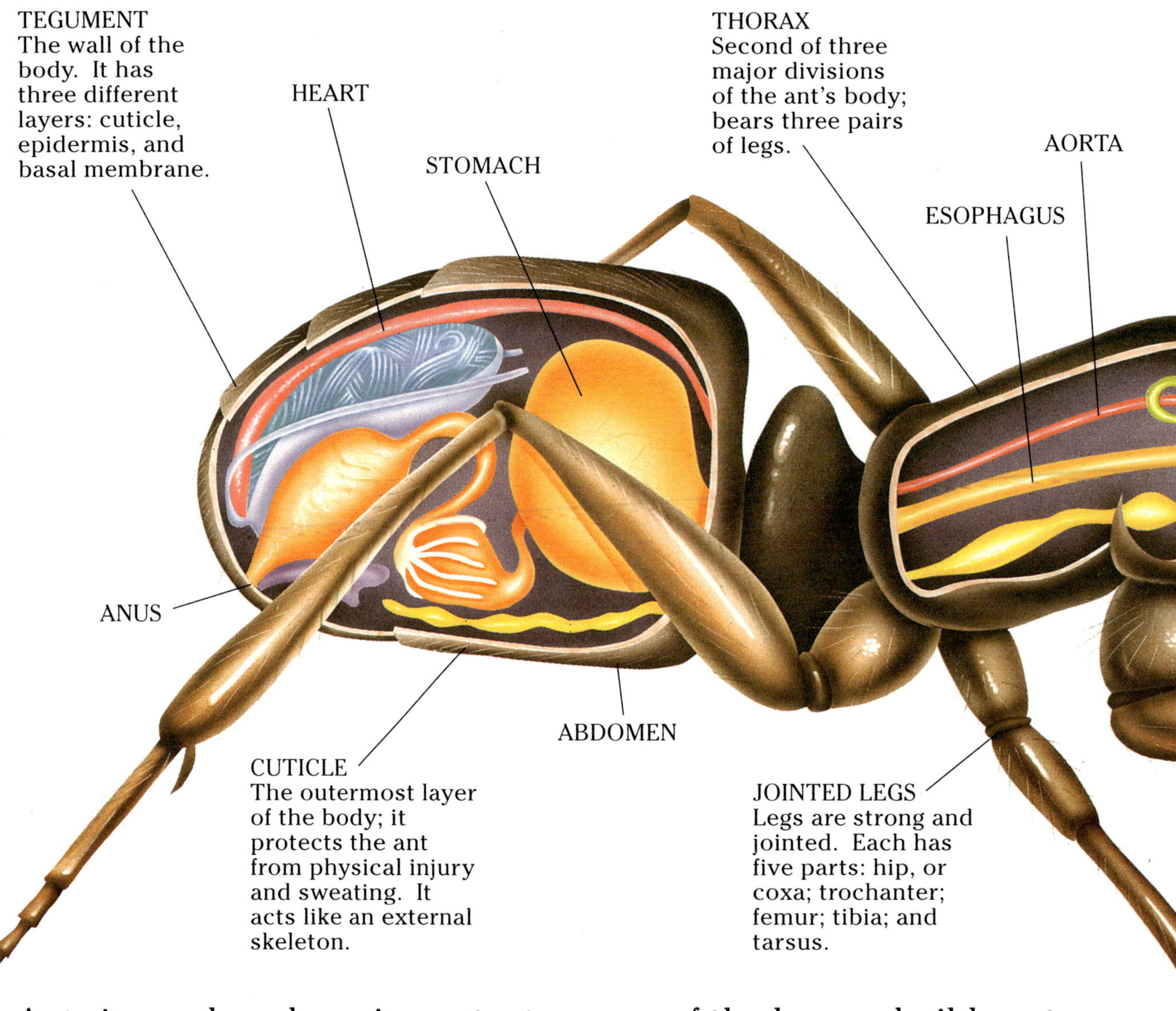

Ants in a colony have important physical differences that reflect the work they must perform. An ant's nest is inhabited mostly by females that have useless sexual organs. These are the workers: they look after the queen, take care of the larvae, build nests, obtain food, and defend the colony. Because of different tasks, the workers come in various shapes and sizes. This illustration shows what a worker ant looks like.

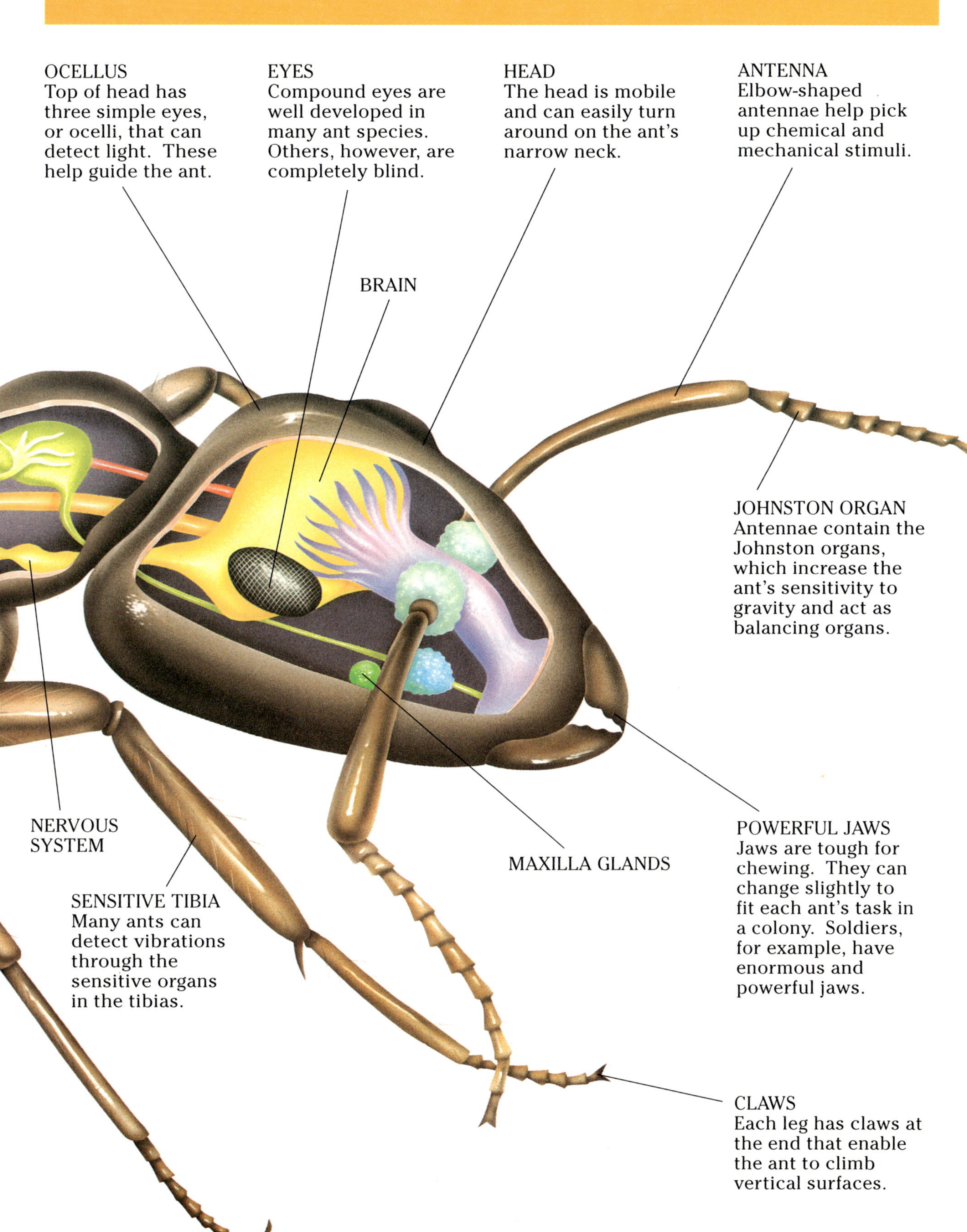

OCELLUS
Top of head has three simple eyes, or ocelli, that can detect light. These help guide the ant.

EYES
Compound eyes are well developed in many ant species. Others, however, are completely blind.

HEAD
The head is mobile and can easily turn around on the ant's narrow neck.

ANTENNA
Elbow-shaped antennae help pick up chemical and mechanical stimuli.

BRAIN

JOHNSTON ORGAN
Antennae contain the Johnston organs, which increase the ant's sensitivity to gravity and act as balancing organs.

NERVOUS SYSTEM

SENSITIVE TIBIA
Many ants can detect vibrations through the sensitive organs in the tibias.

MAXILLA GLANDS

POWERFUL JAWS
Jaws are tough for chewing. They can change slightly to fit each ant's task in a colony. Soldiers, for example, have enormous and powerful jaws.

CLAWS
Each leg has claws at the end that enable the ant to climb vertical surfaces.

IMMENSE CITIES OF ANTS

Sharing the work

Three classes, or castes, exist in an ant colony. These three castes of individuals differ in physical appearance and tasks: the workers, the males, and the queen (more than one queen can sometimes exist in the same colony). The workers are the largest in number and the smallest in size. Some workers are larger than others, and they act as soldiers for the colony. Soldiers have a very large head and very strong jaws. Their main task is to guard and defend the nest. The queen is the most important ant in the colony, since she lays eggs to provide the colony with new ants.

QUEEN
The queen is the largest ant in the colony – up to 0.8 inches (2 cm) long. It can live up to twenty years in certain species.

MALE
Born at the end of summer, winged males mate with the queen during the spring nuptial flight, then die.

WORKER
Tireless workers have a short life, usually from one to three months. Workers of certain species, however, can live up to eight years.

Founding a colony

The nuptial flight and starting a new nest are the most important events of a colony. In early spring, the males and future queens leave the old nest. During flight, each queen mates. Shortly afterward, the males die, and the young queen sheds its wings and chooses a place to lay the eggs of the new colony. For some species, this is a risky time for the queen, since it has no other ants to protect and feed the first larvae. In other species, several extra workers leave the old nest with the queen.

Ants fly only during the spring nuptial flight.

During the nuptial flight, the males mate with the females and then die.

Structure of an anthill

Anthills are complex systems of chambers and tunnels that house thousands, even millions, of ants. The chambers are located at different levels and have specific purposes: a chamber for laying eggs, warehouses for food supplies, chambers for incubating larvae, fungus farms, and more. Ant nests often go down several feet (m), and the interiors are damp. Small ventilation tunnels

The sun first heats up the outer area of the anthill. Then the heat circulates through the rest of the nest.

Ants spend a lot of time keeping the outer walls of the nest in repair and making certain it is in perfect condition.

connect the colony with the
outside. Red ants build large
nests that are partially
underground, with the rest
rising upward. The outer part is
made of earth, leaves, branches,
and other vegetation. Anthills
can sometimes reach 6.5 feet
(2 m) in height and 13 feet
(4 m) in diameter.

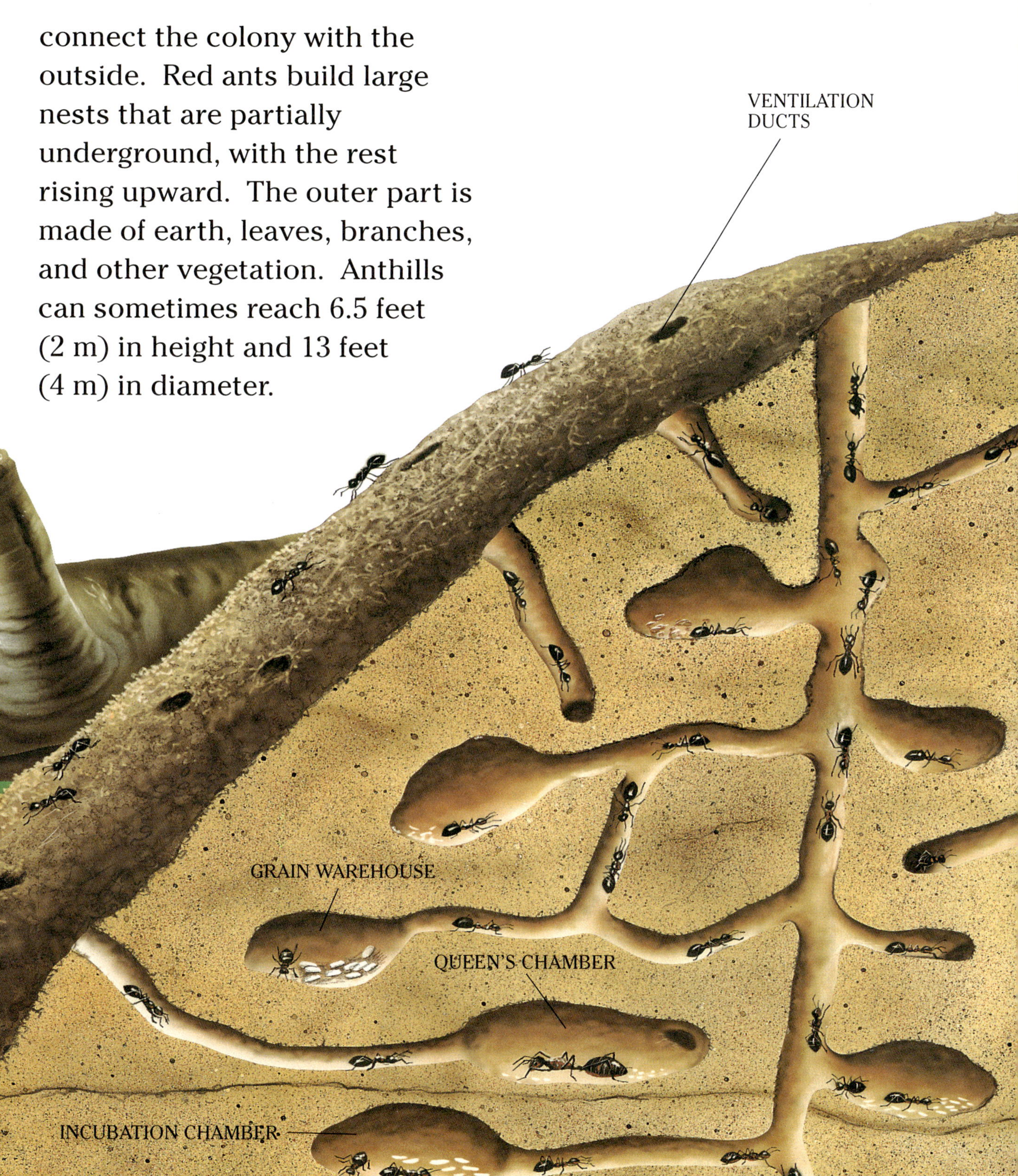

LIVING AND WORKING TOGETHER

An invisible army

The most powerful hunter in the Amazon jungle is the army, or legionary, ant — a small, blind ant that travels along the jungle floor in armies of more than 150,000 individuals. Over 70 different species of army ants exist. Army ants do not have permanent nests. Instead, they spend each night in a different place in a temporary nest made

A "living nest" of army ants has chambers and tunnels in its interior.

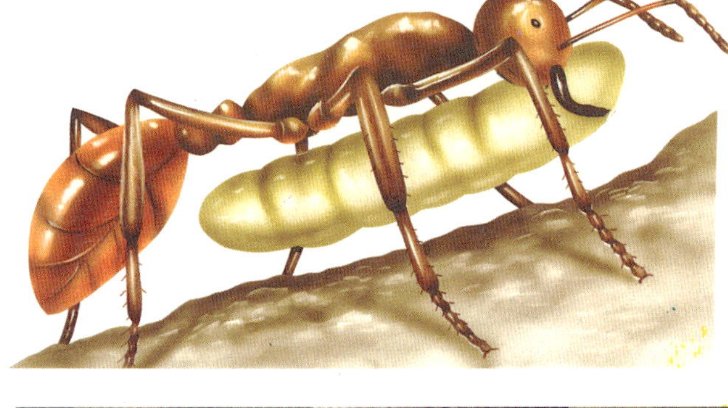

Young workers carry the larvae of the next ant generation between their jaws.

up of the ants' own bodies. Up to 150,000 ants link their powerful legs to create a "living nest" with chambers and tunnels through which other ants can move. The queen stays in a chamber at the nest center. When the army moves, the queen travels in the center with the smallest workers, which carry the larvae. Around them travel the biggest workers, and at the front of the column march the strongest soldiers. The colony moves without stopping for 17 days; then it halts for about 20 days, and the queen lays 20,000 to 30,000 eggs within a week. When the newly-born workers are ready, the army moves out again.

As they move forward, army ants capture all the prey they meet.

Tiny farming ants

Ants are omnivores; they eat animals as well as plants. Certain ant species are such good hunters that they attack larger animals, although they usually attack in a group. Some ant species also like to have a permanent source of food. Leaf-cutting ants, for example, cut leaves into tiny pieces and carry them to the nest. Once inside, the ants chew the leaves into a paste that they use to grow mushrooms. Other species eat honeydew secreted by aphids. The ants protect the aphids in exchange for a few drops of liquid.

When the ant wants a drop of honeydew, it strokes an aphid with its antennae.

Leaf-cutting ants travel to the nest in long columns, each carrying a piece of leaf that is very often much larger than the ant.

that red ants are protected by law?

The red ant is a protected species in many countries. It helps maintain an ecological balance in certain forests. The red ant is such a good hunter that it destroys an enormous number of parasites. In only one year, the members of a medium-sized nest of red ants can capture about 6,100,000 parasites in an oak forest that covers a 0.5-acre (0.2-hectare) area.

ANCESTORS OF THE ANT

The first insects

The first insects appeared on Earth over 400 million years ago. They belonged to the Collembola group, of which 4,000 species survive. None of these insects had wings, but they had special appendages on the fourth of their six abdominal segments that allowed the insects to make huge jumps. These insects normally lived on top of or below damp ground. Up to 700,000 individuals inhabited every 10 square feet (1 sq. m) of rich humus. These animals and their descendants helped change dead vegetation into fertile earth.

The oldest known insect, Rhyniella — only 0.06 inch (1.5 mm).

Gigantic flying insects

A great number of animals quickly began to evolve once Earth had vegetation. Some animals grew to an enormous size, such as the Arthropleura, a centipede over 6.5 feet (2 m) in length.

Among the first large insects was the primitive 8-inch (20-cm) cockroach. At the beginning of the Carboniferous period, about 350 million years ago, a truly impressive winged creature appeared: Meganeura — a huge dragonfly with a wingspan of over 27 inches (70 cm).

Meganeura was the largest winged insect that ever existed.

Primitive insects grew to incredible sizes, such as 6.5-foot (2-m) centipedes and 8-inch (20-cm) cockroaches.

that a colony of army ants can die if its guides get lost?

Army ants are blind, so they must find their way by moving together and using their sense of smell. Each ant leaves a scent that is easily detectable for the one traveling behind. Sometimes the guides become confused and cross the trail made by their own group. Misled by this trail, they start to follow it, and the column ends up walking around in circles. The end is tragic, since the entire colony dies.

THE LIFE OF THE ANT

Growth cycles

Ants go through various stages before they become adults. The queen lays several dozen eggs each year. Workers take care of the eggs in incubation chambers. Each egg hatches one larva that grows for several weeks, shedding its skin, until it becomes a pupa. In most species, the pupa spins a cocoon in which to finish developing. Workers carry the cocoons to warm, dry chambers, where they become adult ants.

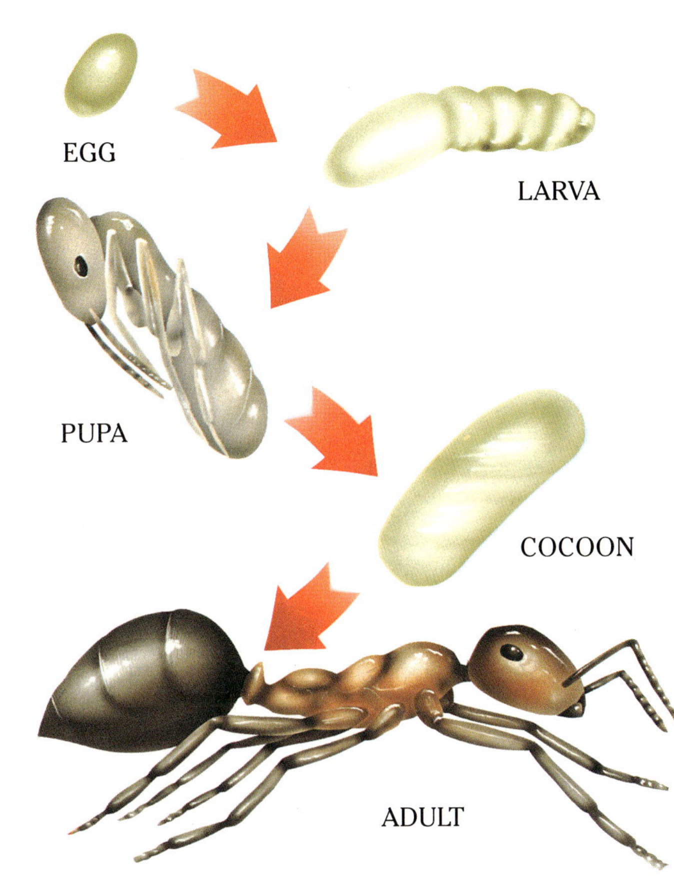

Workers care for the young. The pupae of some ant species do not spin cocoons.

Ant enemies

The ant's worst enemy is the amazing anteater, which thrusts its long and sticky tongue into the nest and devours all the ants that get stuck to it. The anteater's huge appetite can leave a nest almost empty. Spiders, frogs and toads, lizards, chimpanzees, and many species of birds also eat ants. Ants use their strong jaws to defend themselves, although some species also have a poisonous sting for attack and defense.

Ants raise their abdomen to launch drops of poison against enemies.

Some species without a sting have a sac full of poison that they can launch against their enemies from a distance.

The incredible giant anteater, which can measure up to 5 feet (1.5 m) in length and weigh over 45 pounds (20 kg), eats small animals such as ants.

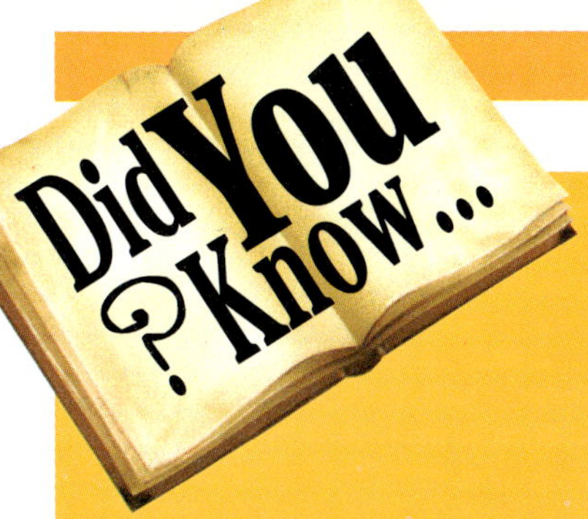

that there are weaving ants?

Not all ants build their nests in the ground. Weaving ants weave tree leaves into a bag. These ants dig their legs into one leaf and draw the next leaf toward the first, using their jaws. Other workers then join the two leaves together, using a thread secreted by the larvae they carry in their jaws. Little by little, the ant nest takes the form of a big hanging bag, which the weaving ants continually repair and enlarge.

APPENDIX TO

SECRETS OF THE ANIMAL WORLD

ANTS
A Great Community

ANT SECRETS

▼ **Ants filled with honey.** Some honey ant workers, also called honeypot workers, fill their abdomen with sugary liquids that they give to other workers. This honey ant hangs itself from the ceiling

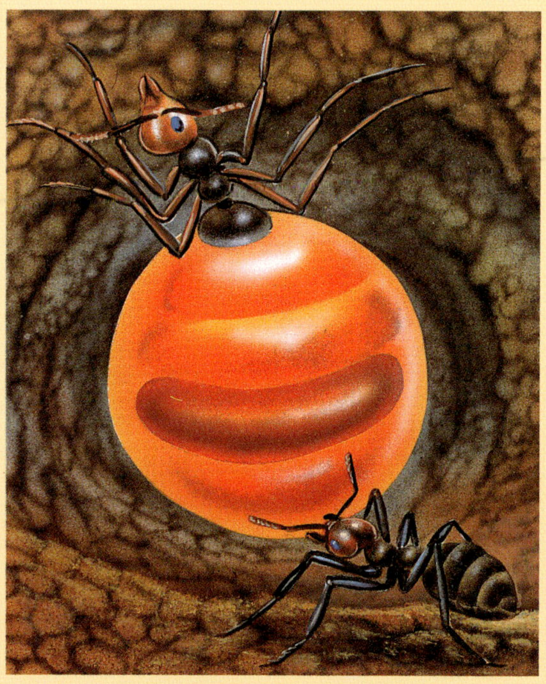

▼ **Nests in trees.** Some ants build their nests in tree trunks. They use their powerful jaws to make tunnels and galleries.

"Milking" caterpillars. Some ants drag live caterpillars into their nests. Caterpillars secrete juices the ants like. To keep the caterpillar alive, the ants feed it young from the nest.

Different eggs. Eggs laid by the queen can be fertilized or unfertilized. Females, both queens and workers, are born from fertilized eggs. Unfertilized eggs become males.

of one of the chambers in the nest. When its hungry companions ask for honey, the honey ant releases some liquid from its abdomen.

Harvester ants. These ants spend the entire warm season collecting grassy seeds that are often much larger and heavier than they are. The seeds are stored in underground grain warehouses inside their huge nests. These nests are in the shape of mounds as large as 20 to 30 feet (6 to 9 m) in diameter and 6.5 feet (2 m) in depth.

1. Ants belong to the order:
a) Lepidoptera.
b) Coleoptera.
c) Hymenoptera.

2. There are more than:
a) 120,000 different species of ants.
b) 8,800 different species of ants.
c) 1,200 different species of ants.

3. After the nuptial flight,
   the males:
a) become workers.
b) lose their wings and migrate.
c) die.

4. The ant is a(n):
a) herbivore.
b) carnivore.
c) omnivore.

5. The Meganeura was:
a) a gigantic prehistoric cockroach.
b) a gigantic prehistoric dragonfly.
c) a gigantic prehistoric centipede.

6. Before becoming adults, the ant
   larvae turn into:
a) pupae.
b) young workers.
c) soldiers.

The answers to ANT SECRETS questions are on page 32.

GLOSSARY

abdomen: the section of body behind the thorax; the rearmost section of an ant. The abdomen contains the digestive organs. Some worker ants have two stomachs in this area, one for the digestive process and one for storing food.

anus: an opening in the body through which waste is excreted.

aorta: the body's main artery that carries blood directly from the heart to other arteries that branch from it.

aphids: also known as plant lice, these insects suck the juices of plants and can cause serious damage to crops. Ants sometimes use aphids as a food supply.

appendages: body parts attached to the main body, or trunk. For example, an insect's legs are appendages.

basal membrane: the innermost layer of an ant's body wall.

Camponotus: the scientific name for carpenter ants. Carpenter ants are black and live in wood.

Carboniferous period: the prehistoric period in which coal beds were formed.

castes: the social divisions in a community.

characteristics: traits or features that separate one object or organism from another. For example, one characteristic of the queen ant is that she is larger than other ants in the colony.

cocoon: a silk casing that an ant pupa spins around itself and in which it develops into an adult.

colony: a community with members that live and work together. Ants are social creatures, and ant colonies can contain hundreds or more insects. Ant colonies can exist in the wood of trees and houses and, most commonly, in soil. Colonies are complex structures with many tunnels and chambers that ants use to store food, grow food, live, and for other purposes.

coxa: the hip section of an animal.

cuticle: the outermost layer of skin that helps protect the body.

environment: the surroundings in which plants, animals, and other organisms live. Ants can live in many different environments, including deserts and mountains.

epidermis: the layer of the ant's body wall between the basal membrane and the cuticle.

esophagus: a tube that connects the throat to the stomach.

femur: the third leg segment from the thorax.

fertile: rich and productive; capable of supporting life and growth.

harvester ants: also known as fire ants, these ants gather seeds from the ground and store them in their colonies below the ground. Harvester ants are careful not to let the seeds sprout by keeping them dry and biting off any sprout that begins to form.

humus: decaying vegetable and animal matter.

Hymenoptera: the scientific order to which ants belong. This order includes more than 103,000 different species.

incubate: to keep eggs warm, usually with body heat, so they will hatch.

larva: the stage in an ant's life cycle that occurs after it hatches from an egg. The larva has a wormlike appearance with partially transparent skin. Larvae are mostly helpless and need full-grown ants to feed, clean, and move them.

nuptial flight: a stage in the ant's breeding cycle when male ants and future queen ants fly away from the nest and mate.

omnivores: animals that eat both meat and plants. Certain species of ants are omnivores.

parasites: organisms that live in or on other organisms.

pupa: the stage in an ant's growth cycle when it is developing inside a cocoon.

sentry: a soldier or guard that watches over an entrance and keeps intruders away. Ant sentries keep enemies or unwanted visitors away from the colony.

stimulus: something that causes a sensation or excitement.

tarsus: the last, or fifth, segment of the ant leg from the thorax. Connected to the tibia, the tarsus is the part of the leg that touches the ground.

tegument: the outer covering or shell that covers the body. In an ant, the tegument is made up of the cuticle, epidermis, and basal membrane.

thorax: the middle of an insect's three body sections. It lies between the head and the abdomen.

tibia: counting from the thorax, the tibia is the fourth leg segment, located between the femur and the tarsus.

trochanter: the second leg segment from the thorax. It joins the femur to the hip.

ACTIVITIES

◆ Find an ant colony outdoors to study. Look in your backyard or local park, checking the open areas as well as under rocks or wood. Watch the colony every day for an hour at different times. Keep a daily journal of your observations. See how weather changes, such as rain, cold, or extreme heat, affect how the ant colony works. Record how far worker ants stray from the colony to find food. Do any predators attack the ant colony? If the colony comes under attack, record how the ants defend themselves.

◆ To observe many different kinds of ants, some of which may not be common to where you live, visit a nearby museum of natural science, an insectarium, or a zoo with insect displays. Most of these places have insect displays that include rare and unusual types of ants.

MORE BOOKS TO READ

An Ant Colony. Andreas and Heiderose Fischer-Nagel (Carolrhoda)
The Ant on the Ground. Linda Losito (Gareth Stevens)
Ants. Patricia B. Demuth (Macmillan)
Ants. Cynthia Overbeck (Lerner Publications)
Eyewitness Explorers: Insects. (Dorling Kindersley)
The Fascinating World of Ants. Maria A. Julivert (Barron)
Insect Attack. Christopher Lampton (Millbrook Press)
Insects. Anita Garner (Watts)
Insects. Jenny Tesar (Blackbirch)
Life of the Ant. Jun Nanao (Raintree Steck-Vaughn)
Looking at Insects. David Suzuki (Wiley)
Some Ants Are Farmers. Alan Silverstein (Lothrop)
Terror in the Tropics: The Army Ants. T. Lisker (Raintree Steck-Vaughn)

VIDEOS

Amazing Ant. (Coronet/MTI Film & Video)
Ant Life. (International Film Bureau)
Fire Ants. (Cornell University)
In Search of Deadly Ants. (Pyramid Film and Video)
A Thousand Million Million Ants. (Carolina Biological Supply Co.)

PLACES TO VISIT

Otto Orkin Insect Zoo
National Museum of
    Natural History
Smithsonian Institution
10 Constitution Avenue
Washington, D.C. 20560

Otago Museum
419 Great King Street
Dunedin, New Zealand

**Metropolitan Toronto
    Zoo**
Meadowvale Road
West Hill
Toronto, Ontario
M1E 4R5

Cincinatti Zoo
3400 Vine Street
Cincinatti, OH 45220

Insectorium of Montreal
4581 Sherbrooke East
Montreal, Quebec
H1X 2B2

Museum of Victoria
222 Exhibition Street
Melbourne, Victoria
Australia 3000

INDEX